The Night Trotsky Came to Stay

For Louise and Arthur

Thanks are due to Peter Carpenter, Jane Draycott, David Morley, Susan Utting; and The Poetry Trust and The Jerwood Foundation.

Some of these poems were previously published in *Envoi, The Interpreter's House, Iota, Mslexia, The North, Obsessed with Pipework, Pique Anthology, Poetry News, Rialto, Room Anthology (Tonbridge Competition Anthology), Seam, Smiths Knoll.*
A selection appeared in *Bedford Square 3: New Writing from the Royal Holloway Creative Writing Programme.*
Interiors won 3rd prize in the Pitshanger Competition 2007.
Allison McVety won the PDF Poetry Prize in 2006.

This collection was the main winner in The Poetry Business Book & Pamphlet Competition 2006.

The Night Trotsky Came to Stay

Allison McVety

Smith/Doorstop Books

Published 2007 by
Smith/Doorstop Books
The Poetry Business
The Studio
Byram Arcade
Westgate
Huddersfield HD1 1ND

www.poetrybusiness.co.uk

ISBN 978-1-902382-90-6

Allison McVety hereby asserts her moral right to be
identified as the author of this book.

British Library Cataloguing-in-Publication Data. A
catalogue record for this book is available from the British
Library.

Designed and typeset at The Poetry Business
Printed and bound by C P I Antony Row e, Eastbourne
Author's photograph by Denis Fowler, Picture Perfect
Studios, Wokingham

Front cover picture: *Still Life with Frying Pan, c. 1954*
by William Scott 1913-1989 (gouache on paper
31.75x27cms). © William Scott Estate 2007.
Image supplied courtesy of Offer Waterman & Co.
Distributed by Central Books Ltd., 99 Wallis Road,
London E9 5LN
The Poetry Business gratefully acknowledges the help of
Arts Council England and Kirklees Culture and Leisure
Services..

CONTENTS

Portrait

My father carried his mother through Yugoslavia
and Greece. Stitched into the lining of his coat

and, against regulations, she kept him company
through the days he hid in back rooms and under stairs;

suckled him on nights huddled in churchyards,
with only the chatter of his pad and key. He folded her

into his wallet, where she rubbed up against
pound notes, discharge papers, a thank-you letter

from General Tito. Around her neck, in miniature,
her brother, on a row of cultured pearls: his face

crimped by the crease of leather. His eyes give no hint
of my mother, though he has her lips. He is his pre-gassed,

pre-shot self. And I am the daughter of cousins, a woman
with no children. I think of losing her in a crowd, slipping her

into someone's jacket, an open bag, that sagging pocket
on the train, for her to live another life, our line travelling on.

Telegram

When it came, she put the envelope,
moth wings still folded, still sealed,
into a box too small to hold a dead-
not-dead man. The lid, worked

from the burl of an oak, is mortise
and tenoned, closed on a blind
hinge. For eighty years he's been missing,
presumed dead, killed in action.

A telegram not read places him
in a war grave, on last parade
and in a field hospital on the fringe
of a battleground healed with grass,

his own scabs a knotty veneer,
his memory lost. This box, a trousseau gift
to tot up the cotton, linen, copper years,
not meant to end with paper,

is never opened, its dowels as raw
as when the bradawl, auger, granny's tooth
had scrawled their marks, its lining spared
the fading light. Imagine a man inside

an envelope, inside a crowded box,
tired of being; imagine lives lived inside out,
of always being a hair's breadth,
a paper-knife, a bayonet slit, from fact.

How you can know a place

and not. How you can know it
through your feet, through the pitch
and crack of pavement, through games:
their stones and sticks,
through hopscotch numbers
scratched on flags with chalk or coal.
Through the clip of ropes on kerbs,
the tap on grids, through the clap of hands,
the toll of dustbin lids, the spark
of studs on boots. Through Messerschmidt
and Spitfire arms, strobed or flecked
with rationed sun. How you can see a thing,
defined through shadows,
the twitch of nets, the very thick of it.
Through the snatch and flare
of two fags lit with the same match,
through the warden's bawl
to *put that bloody light out,*
to *shut the flaming door.* How one shell
can re-shape the place you know,
shift a shelter three feet north,
so you dig for the man in the tin hat
in the wrong place. And how
when they lift your father,
caked in dust, there are no cuts,
no bruises. This is how a man drowns
in earth, this is how you know a place.

Kippers

De-mobbed, you skulk
the day away in
an ill-fitting suit.

In the scullery
you watch her
scale herring
with the edge of a blade.

Sequins attach themselves
to eyelash, to stray hair,
like rain on the night
she said yes.

She slits fish, slides
guts into the slop bucket,
splays them wide to newsprint,
slaps on salt, drops
each fillet into brine.

Later, as she laces jaw to jaw
you remember skulls
row upon row,
then her bottom lip
in your mouth
her raw tongue on yours.

While she hangs each pair
on tenterhooks
in the smoking shed,
you shut the door,
drag from a cigarette, walk
your own smog to the pub.

Ship Canal

Sometimes, they'd ease the bodies
back across the canal,
truncheon them over to Salford.
Only those who'd lagged too long
in the shallows. Bigger than when they went in,
some had been there for months
sucking at silt, threaded through reed beds.
Slipping the bank without being seen,
their last sounds gathered
in the vaults of bridges. I see them:
gold barges oaring their way to Avalon,
feluccas, sails bleached by Ra,
or the final blaze of longboats.
Then, my Uncle Eric saying how,
on the graveyard shift in docklands,
when corpses were dragged ashore,
by men who stuffed their mouths
with rags against the stench,
their colours ran
and they shrank to nothing.

Pediscript

Paving stones were vellum to her shoes,
the soles marked out with chalk
which he'd put there to keep her home.
She had her own stick tucked in reams
of underskirt for days when he had work
and money. And in his stumble
from *The Drummers Arms* to hers,
too blind to read, the street lamps unmasked
her text, and traced the tracks of secret,
calligraphic trips, of market stalls, of shop
fronts filled with other feet, of public gardens,
benches, coach-built prams. Her footsteps,
recto verso leaves, the heel and toe italics
of a promenade, the blotted smudge
of winter treks. And under the make-do-
and-mend of street repairs, the tarmac seal,
her footprints ghost the slabs of Cheetham Hill,
a cobbled sense of how she mapped her days.

Needle Work

She pierces yarn with needles,
sets aside four inches of garter stitch,
walks into the hall where he's fallen,
the worse for bitter and the best of a bottle
of rum, his feet still out on the step,
door open to the frivolity of moths.

She puts a shilling in the slot,
lets last night's supper slow-burn
on the stove again, pulls on her coat,
pauses at the mirror to set her hat,
to slip on gloves, before going to see
the woman who unpicks problems.

Back again she checks his pockets
for the inch of chalk he used to spy,
feels him suck her breath through his teeth,
re-marks the soles of her shoes,
resumes her knitting, picks up the stitch
she'd dropped and waits.

Knitting Patterns

She used oiled Aran the texture of twine,
her index fingers already furrowed
from needles her grandmother had used.
And with the knitting came the yarn:

how she had cabled his sweater with staghorn,
seeded trellis, three braids, honeycomb –
all the same as his father's but changed
the lover's knot for a wishbone –

hoped never to see it, to identify it
pulled from the sea. When it was finished,
mine had a tied cluster and trinity stitch,
but it was the shared patterns my skin

liked most. I wore it on holidays,
on boat trips up the coast and once
I fell asleep against Dad's chest, woke
to find his imprint on my cheek.

The night Trotsky came to stay

she was not best pleased,
refused to let him share her bed,
put him in the box room,
the sheets smelling of must.
She crammed the let-in wardrobe
with all our junk, barricaded the doors,
until like a picket-line it barred the way.
She screwed the windows shut
so there'd be no air, hoped that stifled
as she starched and ironed shirts
he'd go cap-in-hand to some other mug.
All this was lost on him, on strike
at the kitchen table, spare key in his pocket,
a fresh pot on the brew,
newspaper splayed at the jobs page,
spreading his bread thick with butter-tokens
straight from the fridge.

My parents, dancing

So she rolled back the carpet,
mapped out some steps on the red
resin floor; showed him how to grasp
hands, right to left, as if holding
a crane fly, live but captive.
Every Saturday, once I was in bed,
they moved to the sound of the big bands
on the wireless. Only ballroom,
only the basics of quickstep and waltz.
When I can't sleep, I sit at the top
of the stairs, watch them in a spin
or a hesitation turn. Here, with the furniture
back to the wall, they cover the floor,
a couple, always in step with the beat.
And how they would whisk, weave
or chassé, how, with one of the letters
he'd written before they were married
clasped between them, they could dance
a slow foxtrot, not crushing it,
not letting it fall.

Going back to Charlotte Street

I clock them often on the stairs,
in the space between lost and borrowed.
They're flanked by a parlour – reserved

for the dead, where only the boy
with the telegram dares to knock –
and a scullery alive with black-market crops.

She stops on the half-landing, buffs
her neck, scoops a victory wave under the net
with a grip. Their first meeting is sand
through an hourglass, running from her

to him. And I am there too, ghosting the wall,
a smudged image pressed flat on paper,
sifting the grains, watching time and again
the atoms of my own clock forming.

Living up to Ronald Colman

Above the stairs when I come home
after midnight, dancing, he's on duty,
a half-smile balanced with disappointment.
Still in uniform – threadbare by now
if it weren't a picture – he looks like
that actor in the black and white flicks.

I skip the tread of boards mined
with creaks as the quarter chimes snitch
on me. Entrenched, I inch the bannister,
past weighing eyes. This man, gassed
and shot, stands his watch for me,
always expects much more than I am.

On a side ward

my father is trying his death for size.
It's off-the-peg, but even so,
consultants attend to the tailoring,
consider a final tuck. Getting the feel of it,
the weight of the cloth, he tells them
it's heavy across the shoulders;
resigned, before he reads the label,
to wool. It looks too long in the sleeve,
the pockets drown his fists
to the elbow. He opens the jacket
shows me the name in the lining,
asks, *is this really me?*

Swimming Lessons

It rained the whole fortnight,
so my father got it into his head to teach me something useful,
like how to stretch my body out to crawl from doggy paddle,
how to cleave then palm the water, how to skim,
how to drive from the shoulder, the chest, the diaphragm,
how to breathe, regular, on the rim of each third stroke,
and above all how to keep going, to endure the cold,
to enjoy the loneliness, to think of other things besides the swim.

Some days we skiffed the surf with pebbles,
my father's explanations muffled in the hood of a new anorak.
But the gist of his lesson was this: how flat stones are best,
how they have lift, carry on beyond the dunk of lesser ones.

On the one good day, we picnicked on the beach,
my father spoke of how a tanker ran aground on *Pollard's Rock,*
how each successive tide helped retch its guts for miles,
how still, a crude sludge seeps up to meet the press of skin.
I see my mother, how she mops the *Torrey Canyon* from her skirt,
how her lilac handkerchief isn't up to the task.
I hear him say how oil smothered kelp beds,
and the gills of fish were sealed like blackened fingernails.

Tasting the Drink

I am swimming in the sea but you are drowning.
It's the vastness that does for you. Treading water,
the salt reminds you of a different sea,
a different night, when they said they'd come back
under cover of dark, that all you had to do
was hold on. And how you held on, when others
simply stopped, gave in, got the taste for dying.
And they did come back, pulled out the six
who were left from a dozen or more. Since then
you've forgot the delirium of lost faces, forgot
to shun the taste. You have lived your years
on a life-raft, knowing not to drink, but craving something
all the same. Now I am swimming in the sea
and you are drowning. Now the best of them are gone,
you have at last, acquired the taste. You stop.
I crawl my way to shore, look back to where you were.
This taste is on my tongue. It makes me gag.

Brewed-up

And here he stands, at ease,
boots lost in five inches of snow,
smells next door's flooded engine
remembers the stench of '43.
Cordite, the fumes of spilt fuel,
urine, vomit slopped in spent shells,
hung in the air with the ten-day
sweat of a condensed crew.
Outside, shelled Shermans
brewed-up in drifts of hissing sand,
some overturned, full of stewing men.
He gulps from a tin mug
pock-marked sixty years ago,
pisses on crusted snow, strafing
daffodil and crocus shoots.

Time gentlemen, please

Who would wish to sit with the mourning men,
to chivvy the clock; the long wait
pulling at faces, the ratchet click,
the whittle of minutes, pegged
like matches on a cribbage board.
And how the head of a pint drags
the glass, becomes dregs waiting
for the snatch of the pot-man's hand.

These are Legion men, dogged by the smell
of stale slops, of last orders, every year
diminished, reminded of those
who divvied their chits, called time early.
This then their thanatos: a life marked
with what is at hand, ready now for last orders.

The Two Times I Saw your Penis

It slipped from its netting and into view
when I was seven, a dog's tongue
lolling from the leg of your shorts.
The next time: it was in my hand, smaller
than I'd remembered. From a caravan
one week in to the summer holidays
to a bed hours from the end. How then
not to laugh at that accidental flash,
or to think of flaccid and turgid cells
in fifth-form biology, but to keep it steady
against the dish, pretend I'm not holding it,
that you aren't peeing your last; life
running from you, quiet and warm.

Empty

When it's over you'll slip your slow-broiled feet
out of their shoes for the last time, fast-freeze
them on slate tiles, stack them on the rack.

You'll slide open the top drawer of the tall-boy,
pull off each finger, slot them beside your nylons,
handkerchiefs, rouge. You'll lift free your head,

put it in the hat-box, veiled in layers of black,
let it settle with the dust and cracked newspapers
above the wardrobe. Finally, when there is only

a hollowed-out trunk spilled of everything,
you'll pour him into you, as though time is set free
of its glass – be quenched by the loss of him.

Cognitive Development

Remember when we used to spy
number plates through the rear window?
You said that maybe there were no cars,
or people, or trees, or roads, or pylons,

that they only existed
for as long as we looked at them,
if we turned our heads they'd cease to be.
We spent all summer snapping round

to catch the world in its blank-screen state,
not sure what we'd do if the cine film
stopped. I even snapped *you*,
found *you* doing the same to me.

When I heard on the radio
this was just a stage of cognitive development,
I told you. You said you couldn't imagine
saying such a thing.

But I remember. And now, I think
perhaps there's something in it;
that you disappeared because I stopped
sneaking looks to catch you out.

Mapping the World

Mum chose somewhere exotic, out-of-the-way
of the ordinary traveller: the kind who spend their days
on deckchairs, feet in sand; shirt sleeves, trousers, rolled;

the kind who eat luncheon meat sandwiches, take tea
from a flask, stuff the coach with rock, donkeys,
the smell of chips; wanting to pull off at every Services.

It was Bolivia, for us, Syria, Kazakhstan, Reykjavik.
In puppet gloves and elastic-throated pumps we took
the North West Passage; saw whales spurt off the coast

of Alaska, rowed against the current of the Bering Straits;
bathed in the Geysers of Kamchatka; bartered for rice
with buttons, glass beads, with the ribbons from my hair.

Back again, we'd lift the planet off the table, lay place mats
over grain contours, imagine plains, steppes, basins, peaks
rising out of wood, where we ate cold ham with new potatoes,

waited for Dad, the pocket-jangle of his loose-change-tips,
home from a run to Blackpool or Scarborough or Rhyl,
told him our adventures where he slept in front of the box.

Front Door

Our door that yesterday was plum
is undercoat. Each alternate spring
the estate is cloaked in corporation grey.

And home from school, we see it's spread
to drainpipe, railing, garden gate,
as if some early blight has caught us out.

Custard-thick, the top-coats come
in council drab, a uniformity of dun.
But once the gaffer's been to check the job,

she's out with sapphire, emerald,
ruby, gold, paints our door in shades
of special. And home again, we chip

the gloss, are brought up short
by colour, the layers of what she did,
and why she took the trouble.

Outside the Gates at Paxo

I rub sage, picked fresh this morning
into a Pyrex dish, into breadcrumbs,
sausage meat, sweet sweated onions,
bind it with egg and roll into patties
with flattened palms, coil in bacon streaks
or stuff in the neck-end.

I inhale the pepper smell and I'm there,
outside the gates at Paxo
her dress billowing, its pink film on skin.
Hands shade the last ditch of the sun,
draw back high-gloss hair. I taste
the tincture on her lips.

Like arsenic it accumulates under nail
and in curl, marks the three warm months
of summer in 1968 as she packs Paxo
into boxes at the factory. *It's the onions
that make me cry,* she says, as she crosses the road,
contaminates me with the taint.

Pension Day

You push your pension book
under the guillotine trap
of the counter, watch the clerk
stroke each note with the nipples

on his rubber-tipped thumb.
The robber presses his sawn-off
to your neck, the tremor
in his trigger-finger transfers

to the barrel. You tell him
you've been in the WAAF,
that you're *not afraid*
of some cheeky monkey, you know

about the recoil of the Ack-Ack
at the batteries, how to dodge
the high-speed discharge
of empty shells. Afterwards,

you sip sweet tea and the clerk
hands you the book he'd slipped
out of sight of the gunman,
thin with this week's money.

Eighty-seven Hours

> *In terms of flying hours the fighter pilot's life expectancy*
> *[during the summer of the Battle of Britain] could be*
> *measured at eighty-seven.* E. B. Haslam, *Journal of*
> *Strategic Studies* (June, 1981)

She remembers
a young man,
stacked ten chairs high,
asleep,
with eighty-six
hours on his clock
and the bell
about to ring.

It's ringing now
inside her head
at an airfield
pot-holed
by shells
where she walks
on concrete
riddled with grass.

In the moment
between
the movement
of one finger
toward another,
time
congeals
into a single clot.

Taphephobia

Every summer the same: two weeks on the canal
with my uncle and aunt, my berth the aft cabin,
so small it swaddles. At night ropes ache

with the ease of their moorings, the squeeze
of tyre against hull. The ghost
of coal lingers in the grain as the boat stretches

and shrinks in the clink of its skin. I think
of the man on the radio this morning,
how he was born three months too soon,

was placed in a box by a doctor
who didn't think he could live. How his mother
left her bed, crawled the length

of the ward to lift the lid, to raise up this still
living child to her breast. In the lull of a wake
I look through the glass at the layers of silt

that stripe the bank, listen for my own mother
coming to me. Instead I feel the thud of the earth,
the clod that buries me night after night.

Women at their gates

Come summer, the garden gates creaked
against the waiting of women. Down the hall
pans rattle with boiling spuds, the kettle
always on the go. There's cabbage in June,
and in her wrap-around Mrs Walford leans
across the latch. We watch her breasts crest
the shaft of each plank as she hands out
still-warm toffee, fairy cakes, the jubblies
she'd made the day before. How did we get
so far from Foley Walk, the privet hedges,
the crab apple tree, marbles and jacks?
From Mrs Valentine, her twin-sets, pearls,
mock Astrakhan (her Afflecks bargains
concealed inside a Kendall's bag).
From Mrs Sloane's slide from nervous twitch
to Parkinson's. How far from Mrs Dodd
at number four, her Dundee-lilt a foil
to our Mancunian-hard no-nonsense talk.
Far from the women who wait for husbands,
decide when to plate the dinner – eye the clock,
dish out their well-oiled answers
to every question: *Because*; *It's not dark either;*
A run round the table and a bite off the door knob.
How far from Mrs Guttridge in the upstairs flat,
sat behind her hedge on sunny days,
deck chaired, rollered, one eye on the crossword,
one on us, to keep us on the straight and narrow.
How far from Mrs Mac, her walk down
Shadow Moss Road, lab coat open, billowed
with a grand idea. The first to wear a trouser suit
to work, the huff and tut that made her laugh
and echoed round the Walk. We think
we shaped ourselves but it was this mix of women
padlocked to their kitchen lives who taught us
how to wait and what it meant to go.

Boy on the bus

That school gabardine of mine
with its slip-in, slip-out lining,
quilted for winter use,
invisible brown on a bus of standard-issue.
Box-pleats and woollen tights knock knees
with overalls and Crimplene frocks.
In amongst the chiffon,
a crêpe-de-chine square on a shampoo and set.
One man in cavalry-twill, umbrella
tapping a tune on the soles of his brogues. And you
in army & navy surplus, air force blue,
collar raised and cocked, a knapsack
hanging from your shoulder
with the casual cool of *William Hulme*.
I never learned your name or saw you,
beyond your walk to an empty seat,
was never brave enough to look behind
or smile, but I felt you all the same.
Seventeen stops of feeling you.
Boy on the bus, I don't remember what happened
to my gabardine with its slip-in, slip-out lining,
its detachable hood, but I've seen your coat often
at fêtes, in second-hand shops, and once
in the cloakroom of the Festival Hall.
Each time, I've checked the label for your name,
the pockets for mine.

The Knife Thrower's Assistant

                              Three full
rotations, the knife hums on impact,
quivers the wood. It's called a stick
when the blade cleaves the grain,
here it's called a spat or a tiff. His job,
to get the point but dodge
the strike, the knife thrower's
assistant waddles the handle free
of the door, offers it up to his wife,
says, *want to try again?*
                              Overnight
the seam knits, leaves a nick in the paint.

His Theory of String

His world is a cat's cradle
strung from table leg to chair:
particles connected
in one-dimensional chains,
the life he knows snared
with knots he cannot name.

He expands his theory,
tests its limits: darts out
around his father's carver,
the fire irons, the standard lamp,
his mother's sideboard
filled with wedding china,

until it's all connected to him.
Here is his cosmological constant –
snagged with twine and flax –
this, his known universe;
his theory of everything.
He considers other worlds,

the possibility of multiple universes,
each linked to the other.
He loops door handles, waits
to see what happens when chaos
enters his equation, when
the kitchen door is opened,

when gravity steps in, heavy-footed
among the broken plates.
Here the boy sits in his den,
and his theory of string, snapped
by the force, is a child's game,
a theory of nothing.

Interiors

On the day of the Manchester blast
air punched into office blocks –
a thrown fist through a glass wall –
buckled the locks of the filing cabinets,
sucked open drawers, shredded folders
over Market Street, St Anne's Square, the Town Hall.

Deansgate was strafed with claims forms,
the whispers of a thousand rooms
deafened with wine stains, chip-pan fires,
a drop-kick arcing its way
through the greenhouse where an old man
watches *Grandstand* of a Saturday afternoon.

All these interiors mingle in gutters,
buffeted by a now-quiet wind, more drift
than back-draught so that high-rise
shuffles with bungalow, Cheadle Hulme
with Hale Barnes. In the ticker-tape
a crystal vase re-shatters on grid, steals the sun.

And everyone stops to pick up splinters of light,
turning the facets like fresh ideas.
Jack, at the news-stand, rummages in his pockets
for the tube of Airfix he's kept for decades,
in its mangled just-in-case state and a post box
draws its letters close against the aftershock.

All this is a split second's thought.
As though in the still of a bang when paper
and coins are two-facing the sky everything
and nothing is possible. That beautiful time
before the peal of car alarms, the sirens,
the dog bark, the looting of shops.

Union Street

Duck down the alley past stalls
that sell goose eggs and quail,
where red snapper drown in dry air
where mussels, numbed
with crushed ice, mouth help.
Past pre-packed meat, offers
on lamb shanks, offal, burgers,
where skewered kebabs
curled at the corners, sweat
in the heat of midday sun.
Past the nail bar where masked
manicurists, like dentists,
buff, polish, de-scale
the debris of the morning.
Past a boy, his head in the mirror,
mullet moulded with fudge,
with mud from a jar. Past
the key cutters, the cobblers,
where the down-at-heel are bolstered
with a fresh layer of rubber,
where soles are re-glued.
Past shuttered fronts to mangoes,
ripe rimmed, blushed, where plums
tumble at the touch, bruise,
where thin-skinned Jerseys
wait to be rubbed by fingers,
or scraped with the back of a knife.
Down the ginnel, sluice running
the gutter, peel and litter
fighting the current like salmon,
to where a hooded girl sleeps
on cardboard, as squat as a bin bag
as breathless as a fish out of water.

The Gloved Composer

I see you, each hand wrapped in fleece,
standing a little adrift of the check-in queue
at Luxor. Oblivious to luggage, you glide
the concourse, neck braced in stocking stitch,
a full head's height above the galabayas,
the starched linen scarves. I want to peel off
those gloves, expose your pores to sweat.
I want ridges and troughs to breathe, hair
to quiver with the blind alphabet of pharaohs,
to hear their overtures in your palms.
But I don't. I watch you sail past, sterile,
unmoved by quavers and missed chords.
I think of you at your piano, stretching for keys,
your fingers keeping clear of flat notes.

Meat Market, Sham Shui Po

The too-close smell of the metro,
oil drums fired-up as ovens, vats of stock
for hanging birds, absurd in their nudity.

Men in smeared vests drag on cigarettes
while obtuse-angled women tap cages
shoe-horned with chickens and ducks,
to liven them up in their feathers.

As they waited with hungry dogs
for the market to open, she was moved on
by a prostitute, marking her patch
in white plastic shoes, enamel makeup.

He wheels out his story with Bendicks
for dinner-party friends. She smiles
as he slaps her arse, feels the meat.

Jellyfish of Skerry Sound

Contact lenses eye
the clouds, gleet held
convex, turgid with surface
tension. Tie-dyed,
kidney-coloured, insides

kaleidoscopes. A girl
kicks sand at them.
You watch her drill one
with a stick, stand idle
as it weeps rose quartz

and she attacks the next,
thrusts a stake through
pink innards, hits rock.
It makes her fingers tingle
like a tuning fork.

Helsinki

It's four o'clock – someone's painted the sky
with bitumen. Snow pummels
the windscreen, we drive at 80 km an hour,
wipers skating over thin ice: my driver
places too much faith in snow chains.

The dashboard says it's minus 20, I think
it's lying – breath can be sliced, even in cars.
When we stop I see lunatics gathering
in shirt-sleeves, huddled under the canopy
of a long moon, smoking roll-ups.

If I survive the journey I'll eat the herring
the waiter offers me in his ice-white coat
in the dining room; I'll drink water,
retire, listen to the sound
of people climbing walls.

Passing for normal

How quick to slip from lover's hands
to surgeon's; from ardent press
to urgent, examination-room precise.
Here is the turning point.

Sex now is an impossible thought,
an unsuitable gift and you wonder
if there's any going back
or any going forward.

A time perhaps when you might have
the sort of sex that corks a row,
the sort that sands the rough
off a bad day brought home:

the casual currency you used
for love. From this point on
it's serious, as serious as first-time new,
as serious as last-time kind.

No in-between ordinary,
no lying back, no England.
And this malignancy haunts beyond
the wards, the drip-feed,

the day after tomorrow. It will lie
between you, a bolster in your bed,
stinking of sympathy, and the shadow
of it will grow mean with spite.

Tables

Everything breathes again
The tablecloth is white
René Cazelles

i *Setting*

Gone with the dark, he hands back my garden.
No change of the guards, no ceremony, just
a slip-of-the-hand from him to me. The ring-pull
from a cider can hooplas the grass and a light frost
traces his form on the swing. He's slept here again,
under the oaks where the bats nest. And while you
sleep on, I curve myself to his shape, try to work out
what he sees of the sky through the canopy of leaves.

And it's easier, sometimes, lying where he lies than it is
lying beside you. While this displaced man harries
the seasons with his route-march, you wake, find me
watching pond skaters, or the green woodpecker
searching the lawn for grubs and we sway together,
awkwardness slicing the hush like a spade.

*

Slicing the clay, I take the leg clean off a frog.
From the kitchen window you don't see
its struggle to move, just the arch of my back,
come over the wet grass to where I'm crouched.

We don't have the conversation about whether
Frogs' legs grow back like other amphibians',
like newts' legs grow back, because it's too close
to the conversation about hearts.

So you lift the spade, bring it down hard.
With your fingers on my shoulder, we look at the frog,
how it has collapsed in on itself. I am still watching

as you cross the grass again, this time with tea,
in a mug my father would have used, and the heart
almost does flicker with something, like something like hope.

ii *Siding*

Bats lift crane flies from the lawn,
easy pickings on nights like this. The table
is crowded with empty plates and the glasses
are laced with lipstick and dregs.

A napkin under the chair, once crisp, now looks
like it's had the stuffing knocked out of it.
We drink the pot dry. I think of marigolds,
the washing up, you look across the mess to me.

And just when I think you'll spoil it with a bit
of Eric Clapton, or *shall we brick-up the serving hatch?*
you say instead, *come up to bed, we'll sort this out tomorrow.*

Somewhere out on the common land, a hare
screams, but we've already closed the door,
left the night to those who'll use it well.

*

Dawn is the breath between shifts.
The vixen, thin from nursing her cubs
weaves herself between the twisted
hawthorn and the rhododendrons.
No kill tonight, just a scavenge of bins.
But at dawn when she has skimmed
beneath the shed, the birds clock-in
with chimes and pings.
                    They still get it,
everyday, they still get the point of dawn,
even with red suns, with magpies gathered
in next door's spruce like it's 6pm and nothing's
coming but bad news. And they sing
because what else can they do with the light,
the cold air, the breath that gives them lift.

Bronze Age Skull

A woman's skull in my hands,
it's the pinking shear seam
I notice first. Emptied,
forehead thick with the silt
of calcification, the bone porous,
honeycombed, ounces balanced
in my fingers. In the upper jaw,
the roots of an incisor travelling
north and the tell-tale borehole
shaped by the thrust and gnaw
of a tumour. And it occurs to me
with others' hands cradling,
cupped against accidental fall,
that her head, hollow, carries
more weight than mine.

Hardy's Grandmother tells him how she heard
the news of the French Queen's death

Perhaps he enjoys the telling,
how peeled-back smooth she is
as she recalls the iron's track
across her one good frock, muslin,
folds unwrapping in the heat,
the pattern re-printed in her head
with each remembering. Her hands
press the shift and weave of air
and years between them. The oven
burns furze, the dough pulls
at its own skin to come to bread.
And how still she stands at news
of the beheading, licks her finger,
quells the sudden burn, eases
the collar into place. Her hands
fret a pucker at the neck.

Diving

You're a passenger before you're launched
through the windscreen, lose *Woman's Hour*,
enter the air; the splinters of words, the tinnitus
of glass come with you, blisters of breath
thrust into a pool at the end of a dive, hooked
on your skin, to cling then break, resurface,
and it's here you attend

                              to posture, to style,
level of difficulty; and on the tarmac
the grey mosaic spattered black with rain,
while everyone runs to your crossroads to look
at the gape in the laminate craze; and it's here
you learn from your mistake, step through each frame,
speak its dimensions, remember its shape.

Harris Hawk

At first ordinary brown, school-uniform brown,
the brown you imagine your mother to be
on the inside on one of her browned-off
ironing days. A nothing-special bird,

claws and beak inert, hawked on the arm of a pimp
and traded from building top to building top.
Weight balanced between hunger and instinct
is the difference between hunter and killer.

Dressed in the tat of a full-moult coat,
at a word this hen is amber and jet, a tiger-eye glint
and flushed with a slip of petticoat-white,
white camisole on a washing line white.

She lifts from his grip, is raised to warrior queen
in a Boudicca cloak, sings her yawp to the man
in the anorak. He dances to the tune of her bells
and she has him in the palm of his own hand.

Saxon Tree Boat

Parched, this oak dissolves to dry-cure state,
pulls back from paddle and pole
as if boat was just a phase. There's the riddle
of fractures on the hull, the fox and char
of centuries. Here, and here, the grain flexes,
compresses, flails against the soak and thirst;
this mottle of time becomes its own landscape,
a riverbed run arid. The shivers
of this tree could be ice-floes, fingerprints,
or evolution in reverse-frame;
its shrinkage a reflex action,
or because it's been sucked free of its river,
is crazed with the grief of it.

Under Trees

I want to tell you something about your beads:
cobalt and nimbus; earth strung next to earth.
I think of parallel worlds while you warm your hands.

They lie in the basin of your collar bone, these globes,
turn on an axis of thread and as you lean
to where I'm sitting on the bed, they free wheel

in space. On one of these other worlds that hangs
at your neck, I might be walking under trees
that sound like water on the way to the sea,

I might be dancing at the Ritz. If I snapped the string,
let loose the planets, I'd scoop up a different life, exchange
the sphere under your fingers for the one in my hand.

Still Life

William Scott RA (1913-1989)

In Scott, absence is always the thing to cling to.
It hangs in the air, an echo draped on a hook
behind the door, where a coat should be. But look again –
the pan is not cold, the fish are not wasted.
What's not there affects what is. We are caught between
frames, where something has happened, something will happen.
In this moment of ordinariness, the furniture rests
back into itself and you might almost miss the shape of him,
how he lingers in the hole he made when he left;
not actually painted, but residual in the load
of the paint, like he's stepped out into the yard to hush
the dog that barks at the cat. He'll come back, break eggs,
watch the transparent glaze to white, splash the yolk
with lard, eat straight from the pan so as not to spoil
tomorrow's composition. The yellow will run, paled
at the touch of hot fat, but still yellow on black on black –
the layers of old ground that season the pan.